God's World of Animals

by Heno Head, Jr.
illustrated by Rusty Fletcher

To John and Ruth

© 2002 Standard Publishing, Cincinnati, Ohio. A division of Standex International Corporation. All rights reserved. Sprout logo and trade dress are trademarks of Standard Publishing. Printed in the United States of America. Project editor: Laura Derico. Cover design: Suzanne Jacobson.
ISBN 0-7847-1395-2

08 07 06 05 04 03 02   9 8 7 6 5 4 3 2 1

Standard
PUBLISHING
CINCINNATI, OHIO

God made a whole wide wonderful world of ANIMALS. Animals run on land, climb in trees, fly through air, and swim in seas. They are everywhere. They bark, purr, moo, hoot, tweet, oink, growl, and howl. Some even ROAR!

FISH live in water. God gave fish everything they need. They have bones for shape, fins for swimming, and GILLS for breathing. Gills are perfect for taking air in from the water.

Fish that live in lakes have dark colors, such as deep blues and greens. But many ocean fish are brightly colored—red and yellow, orange and blue, even pink and purple!

Some ocean animals don't have BONES to give them strength, to protect them, or to help them move. But God didn't forget about them! Oysters have hard shells. Lobsters and crabs grip with pinchers. Jellyfish have tiny stingers for protection. Both the squid and octopus wriggle their squiggly arms to move in the water. And starfish crawl upon the ocean sand.

Have you ever seen shells on the beach? Those are the houses of small, soft sea animals. Their shells help to keep them safe. Seeing the pretty shells reminds me of the beautiful home God has made for us in heaven — where we will always be safe!

God made some animals that live in the water and on land — AMPHIBIANS (am-FIB-ee-uns). Amphibians spend the first part of their lives in the water, then later move onto land. Frogs, toads, and salamanders are all amphibians. Have you ever held a frog in your hand?

Can you see the tadpoles swimming in this jar of water? Tadpoles are baby frogs. They have gills now, but in a few weeks they will breathe with lungs. And their tails will get smaller.

Many animals live in warm swamps. Swamps are full of weeds, soggy land, and mucky old water. Swamps are mainly muddy, muddy, muddy.

Alligators and crocodiles are both reptiles. Other reptiles are snakes, turtles, and lizards. Reptiles have skin with scales. Their body temperature changes with the heat of the air. So reptiles may be hot, cold, or just right!

Baby reptiles hatch from eggs. Fish and amphibians do, too.

Baby birds also hatch from eggs. Soon they leave their nests to soar over our heads. BIRDS are the only animals with feathers. They also have hollow bones. Wings, feathers, and hollow bones help birds fly through the air.

Some birds cannot fly. But God helps them do other things well. An ostrich, the largest of all birds, is very fast. It can run across the African plains at speeds up to forty miles an hour. This is faster than the fastest person on earth.

Penguins can't fly, but they can swim. They dive for fish in the cold, cold waters near the South Pole.

On the sixth day of creation God made land animals. That was a great day on earth! Many land animals are MAMMALS. They have coats of fur or hair for staying warm. Mammals walk on four legs. And the mothers give birth to babies that are not in eggs.

If you have a pet, it may be a mammal. Dogs, cats, and hamsters are all mammals.

Some mammals are pets, but others live in the wild. Africa is home to many wild animals. Monkeys swing high through jungle trees. Down below, leopards prowl in the thick forests. Farther up the misty mountainside a family of gorillas searches for fruit and leaves.

Lions, giraffes, and zebras all live on the open grasslands of Africa. Rhinos and elephants also roam these plains in search of food. A roly-poly hippopotamus sloshes in a nearby river. In other areas, camels shuffle across the hot desert sands. Africa is full of all kinds of beautiful mammals that God made.

Some mammals are found only in Australia. Kangaroos spring across the Australian grassland in great leaps. Many can jump over 25 feet in one hop! Mama kangaroos carry their little "joeys" in pouches. Pouched mammals are called MARSUPIALS (mar-SOO-pea-uls).

Another Australian is the koala (ko-wah-la). This little mammal spends its life in trees, eating leaves, and posing for pictures. Koalas have pouches, too. They are marsupials, not bears.

Mammals have even traveled to faraway cold places. Polar bears and arctic foxes live in the frozen north. Seals dive for fish in the icy water. Brrrrr.

Blue whales like to swim in the cold waters, too. These sea mammals are the largest animals on earth. Other ocean mammals are dolphins and porpoises (POR-puh-ses). Sea mammals have fins or flippers for swimming. All of them breathe with lungs, so they must come to the surface for air.

Many mammals live in the forests. The trees and brush give them food and hiding places. Look closely. Can you find the squirrel and raccoon? How about the beaver on his dam and the bear fishing in the stream? What other animals do you see? (rabbit, fox, and white-tailed deer)

Some animals, such as this giant panda bear, are ENDANGERED. There are only a few of these bears left in the whole world. Many other animals are also endangered. If we want to enjoy them, we have to help them to live in this world.

In that way, we can say thank you, God, for your wonderful world of animals.